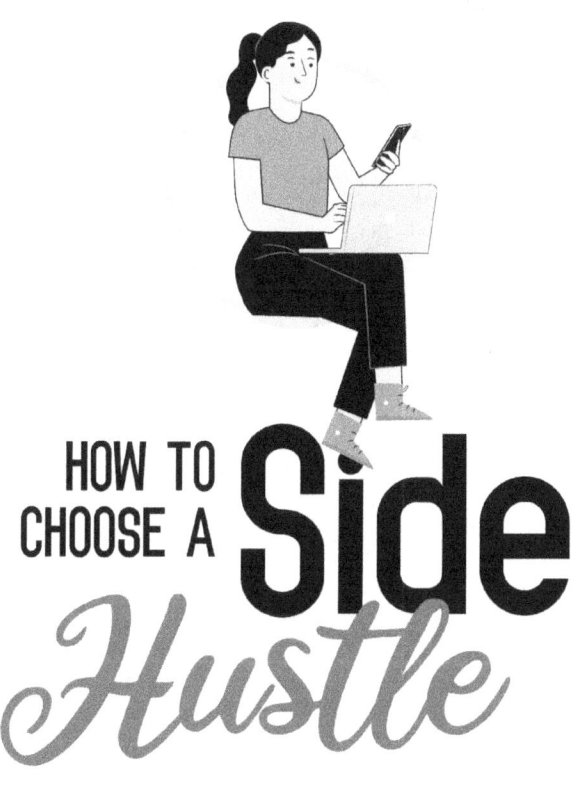

HOW TO CHOOSE A Side Hustle

6 STEPS TO DESIGN A STARTUP BUSINESS FOR A HAPPY, SUCCESSFUL & PURPOSE DRIVEN LIFE

TurtlePublishing

Published by Turtle Publishing
All rights reserved.

Printed on demand in Australia, United States and United Kingdom.

Written & designed by Kathy Shanks
© Kathy Shanks 2021
Illustrations by Freepik Storyset & Turtle Publishing

No part of this publication may be reproduced, stored in a retrieval system, or transmitted in any form or by any means, electronic, mechanical, photocopying, recording or otherwise, without the prior written permission of the author.

Under no circumstances will any blame or legal responsibility be held against the publisher, or author, for any damages, reparation, or monetary loss due to the information contained within this book including, but not limited to — errors, omissions, or inaccuracies. Either directly or indirectly. You are responsible for your own choices, actions, and results.

Legal Notice: This book is copyright protected. This book is only for personal use. You cannot amend, distribute, sell, use, quote or paraphrase any part, or the content within this book, without the consent of the author or publisher.

Disclaimer: Please note the information contained within this document is for educational and entertainment purposes only. All effort has been executed to present accurate, up to date, and reliable, complete information. No warranties of any kind are declared or implied. Readers acknowledge that the author is not engaging in the rendering of legal, financial, medical or professional advice. The content within this book has been derived from various sources. Please consult a licensed professional before attempting any techniques outlined in this book.

SPECIAL BONUS

FREE Workbook including Journaling Activities for choosing your Side Hustle PLUS over 120 Inspirational Books to add to your Reading List

Get FREE unlimited access to this AND all of my new books by joining our fan base!

SCAN WITH YOUR CAMERA OR GO TO
bit.ly/SideHustleWorkbook

TABLE OF CONTENTS

ABOUT THE AUTHOR   vii
INTRODUCTION   ix

STEP ONE

Discover you   1

What are your values?	2
What are you passionate about?	10
What is your purpose?	12
What would make you happy?	14

STEP TWO

Consider what you want   17

Who do you want to spend your time with?	18
What schedule do you want to work?	19
What skills can you capitalise on?	21
How do you want to give back?	22
What can you learn from the past?	24

STEP THREE

Understand your options   29

Trading hours for dollars	29
Passive income	31
Network Marketing	33

STEP FOUR
Overcome your obstacles — 37

Fear	38
Money and time	40
Procrastination	41
Imposter Syndrome	42
The people around you	44
Belief in yourself	45

STEP FIVE
Make some decisions — 49

How much time can you commit?	50
What's the long-term goal?	52
What types of hours do you want to work?	52
What does success look like to you?	54

STEP SIX
Follow the leaders — 57

Your mindset is the key	58
Get out of your own way	59
Take time out for yourself	60
Don't ignore your relationships	61
You don't have to be unique	61

Final words — 65

REFERENCES — 69

ABOUT THE AUTHOR

Kathy Shanks is a businesswoman and entrepreneur, as well as a wife of 18 years and a mother of two. She has been self-employed for over twenty years and started three businesses from the ground up. She sold one during COVID's peak, and she is still managing the other two. Not only that, but Kathy is a firm believer that anyone can do anything they set their mind to. Her favourite quote has always been, "you can because you think you can." She believes we all deserve to live our best lives. We all deserve to work in a career the fulfils our heart, mind, body and soul.

Many years ago, while attending a very intense personal development event, she was incredibly inspired to make some changes in her life. It was the sort of content that gives you that 'light-bulb moment' we always hear about. She thought to herself, *why did I not hear this 20 years ago?* As she was thinking this, the lady who was sitting next to her said, "I wish I'd heard this 20 years ago."

Kathy looked up at her for the first time since they'd entered the room. Her mind was blown for the second time in as many minutes. The lovely lady who felt the need to say this out loud was approximately 20 years older than her. A few things hit Kathy all at once. Firstly, she realised with relief that she still had time. Secondly, the reality is that she probably did hear something like this 20 years ago. But she wasn't ready to really 'hear' it and take it on board. Thirdly, she wondered, *what am I not hearing now that perhaps in 20 years I wish I had listened to?*

Since then, Kathy has filled her mind with as much personal development content as her brain could handle. She loves learning new things, but she wanted more than just the information. She wanted to take action. That's when she started developing her own method of journaling. This process has allowed her to understand herself and create a working environment that adheres to many of the principles you will read in this book.

Kathy has chosen to never settle for mediocre when it comes to her career. We spend so much of our lives working; it should be something that fulfils us every day, rather than something we tolerate to pay the bills. Kathy decided long ago that working on her terms was the most important aspect of her working life, so she created her businesses to suit her needs. She's often told, "you're lucky to be able to work at home." There's no luck involved! You are the creator of your lifestyle, and this book is the process in how she's done that.

Are you ready to create your side hustle? Then let's go. Time to learn about you and how you can create your perfect side hustle.

INTRODUCTION

" Your time is limited, so don't waste it living someone else's life. Don't be trapped by dogma – which is living with the results of other people's thinking. Don't let the noise of others' opinions drown out your own inner voice. And most important, have the courage to follow your heart and intuition. They somehow already know what you truly want to become. Everything else is secondary."
– Steve Jobs

Imagine going on a tropical holiday, finally purchasing new furniture for your home, hiring a chef, or buying your dream car. These don't have to be fictional scenarios in your head. All of this can be attainable by creating your own side hustle!

A side hustle, at one time, meant earning a few extra bucks outside of your daytime job, but the definition has broadened, as many have successfully turned their side hustles into full-blown businesses. The popularity of the side hustle has witnessed a spike in recent years. A 2017 study from Bankrate concluded that more than 44 million Americans have a side job, ranging from freelancing projects to being a part of a gig economy world.

So why is everyone so keen on starting a side hustle?

Building a side hustle income is a stepping stone towards financial freedom. It allows you to direct your focus on what you are most passionate about, while simultaneously giving you flexibility and more money in your bank account. Additionally, you earn for yourself instead of a corporation. You become the boss of your income and do not have to wait for payday to take your kids to their favourite amusement park. We all daydream of freeing ourselves from the shackles of a 9-5 job, and a side hustle that has the potential to turn into a full-time career can provide just that!

I know how easy it is to get bored by the monotony of life, to let the daily routine take over and settle its claws into you. You can end up apathetic and lacking the energy to focus on yourself, your loved ones, and your hobbies. Despite pouring all of your energy into your job, it rarely rewards you as you deserve. While starting your own business from scratch sounds like a huge leap, imagine working from home, in comfortable clothing, being your own boss, working the hours of your choice and setting your own pay rate.

I'm assuming you have been dreaming about this for a while. You may have done some research into side hustle options and chatted with friends about what they think, and yet you still feel stuck. Sure, starting a side hustle sounds **AMAZING**, *but what can I do?* You have probably watched several videos by YouTube 'gurus' who narrate their own experience, persuading you that *starting a side business of candle-making is honestly the best thing that has ever happened to them*. While this may be true for them, you should not be looking into the candle business if it is not an activity that appeals to your personality. There are hundreds of side hustles, and plenty that will fit your interests perfectly. Search within yourself, find what suits you, and take the leap. If you follow your passion, it will not only lift your energy, but drive you to work even harder. This hard work will manifest itself in what you do, positively influence your clients, and eventually ensure that your business will flourish.

This book aims to clear your confusion and help you discover the perfect side hustle for you. If you don't know where to begin, or perhaps have fifty ideas, and you're unsure which direction to follow, you have picked up the right book. Prepare to embark on a journey to discover the best side hustles, the ones that resonate with your body, heart, mind and soul.

STEP ONE
Discover you

STEP TWO
Consider what you want

STEP SIX
Follow the leader

STEP THREE
Understand your options

STEP FIVE
Make some decisions

STEP FOUR
Overcome your obstacles

STEP ONE
Discover you

"One of the huge mistakes people make is that they try to force an interest on themselves. You don't choose your passions; your passions choose you." **– Jeff Bezos**

The journey to success begins with discovering yourself. Take a deep look within yourself, discover where your true strengths and weaknesses lie, understand your wants and needs, and use that knowledge to begin down the path that you deem the best one for you. Every individual on this planet is cut out for something, and we're all different. What's good for the goose is not good for the gander. Every individual is passionate about something. You may already know your passion. If not, this chapter will begin the process of giving you clarity on the age-old question, **"Who am I."**

What are your values?

To live a life of harmony and peace, you need to define what your personal values are. Values are vital to your being, forming the foundation of your personality by motivating and guiding you towards certain decisions. These values include the traits and characteristics you grew up with and may be influenced by various factors, including family, culture, environment, society, religious beliefs, and ethnicity.

In order to succeed in life, you need to understand your values and how to use those to shape your life.

Perhaps you are the kind of person intimidated by the thought of directly interacting with others. Therefore, you prefer a quiet workplace with few co-workers. Or maybe you yearn for an environment that is fast-paced, full of challenges and unpredictability.

You may have jumped into your current career with enthusiasm, believing it was the right job for you. But then, the day-to-day operations didn't live up to your expectations. Maybe you realised that you still want to pursue the field you're in, but on your own terms. Having a deep understanding of your values is the best way to start down this road. Your values bring out your strengths while simultaneously opening your eyes to the weaknesses holding you back.

Get yourself a notebook and pen. Keep this notebook handy as we'll be using it, and referring back to it, throughout the book. Sit down and answer the following questions. The answers will help you to begin the discovery of what makes you who you are.

STEP 1: DISCOVER YOU

Don't overthink it. Think of the first answer that pops into your head and write it down. The answers are within you, and we're going to bring them out.

Journal Activity 1

1. Go through the list of values on the following pages and note each one that is important to you.

2. Now go through your short-list again and write down the top 12 that are most important to you.

3. Go through your list one more time and write down your top 6. Number 1 should be the most important, and number 6 should be the least.

Write out these top 6 on a sheet of paper and put it somewhere you will see it every day – especially as you read through this book. Ensure all your future decisions are compatible with this list. This list is YOU – these are your core values, and any further decisions you make should be reflected in this list.

***

- Abundance
- Acceptance
- Accessibility
- Accomplishment
- Accuracy
- Achievement
- Acknowledgement
- Activeness
- Adaptability
- Adoration
- Adroitness
- Adventure
- Affection
- Affluence
- Aggressiveness
- Agility
- Alertness
- Altruism
- Ambition
- Amusement
- Anticipation
- Appreciation
- Approachability
- Articulacy
- Assertiveness
- Assurance
- Attentiveness
- Attractiveness
- Audacity
- Availability
- Awareness
- Awe
- Balance
- Beauty
- Being the best
- Belonging
- Benevolence
- Bliss
- Boldness
- Bravery
- Brilliance
- Buoyancy
- Calmness
- Camaraderie
- Candor
- Capability
- Care
- Carefulness
- Celebrity
- Certainty
- Challenge
- Charity
- Charm
- Chastity
- Cheerfulness
- Clarity
- Cleanliness
- Clear-mindedness
- Cleverness
- Closeness
- Comfort
- Commitment

STEP 1: DISCOVER YOU

- Compassion
- Completion
- Composure
- Concentration
- Confidence
- Conformity
- Congruency
- Connection
- Consciousness
- Consistency
- Contentment
- Continuity
- Contribution
- Control
- Conviction
- Conviviality
- Coolness
- Cooperation
- Cordiality
- Correctness
- Courage
- Courtesy
- Craftiness
- Creativity
- Credibility
- Cunning
- Curiosity
- Daring
- Decisiveness
- Decorum
- Deference
- Delight
- Dependability
- Depth
- Desire
- Determination
- Devotion
- Devoutness
- Dexterity
- Dignity
- Diligence
- Direction
- Directness
- Discipline
- Discovery
- Discretion
- Diversity
- Dominance
- Dreaming
- Drive
- Duty
- Dynamism
- Eagerness
- Economy
- Ecstasy
- Education
- Effectiveness
- Efficiency
- Elation
- Elegance
- Empathy
- Encouragement

- Endurance
- Energy
- Enjoyment
- Entertainment
- Enthusiasm
- Excellence
- Excitement
- Exhilaration
- Expectancy
- Expediency
- Experience
- Expertise
- Exploration
- Expressiveness
- Extravagance
- Extroversion
- Exuberance
- Fairness
- Faith
- Fame
- Family
- Fascination
- Fashion
- Fearlessness
- Ferocity
- Fidelity
- Fierceness
- Financial independence
- Firmness
- Fitness
- Flexibility
- Flow
- Fluency
- Focus
- Fortitude
- Frankness
- Freedom
- Friendliness
- Frugality
- Fun
- Gallantry
- Generosity
- Gentility
- Giving
- Grace
- Gratitude
- Gregariousness
- Growth
- Guidance
- Happiness
- Harmony
- Health
- Heart
- Helpfulness
- Heroism
- Holiness
- Honesty
- Honor
- Hopefulness
- Hospitality
- Humility
- Humor

STEP 1: DISCOVER YOU

- Hygiene
- Imagination
- Impact
- Impartiality
- Independence
- Industry
- Ingenuity
- Inquisitiveness
- Insightfulness
- Inspiration
- Integrity
- Intelligence
- Intensity
- Intimacy
- Intrepidness
- Introversion
- Intuition
- Intuitiveness
- Inventiveness
- Investing
- Joy
- Judiciousness
- Justice
- Keenness
- Kindness
- Knowledge
- Leadership
- Learning
- Liberation
- Liberty
- Liveliness
- Logic
- Longevity
- Love
- Loyalty
- Majesty
- Making a difference
- Mastery
- Maturity
- Meekness
- Mellowness
- Meticulousness
- Mindfulness
- Modesty
- Motivation
- Mysteriousness
- Neatness
- Nerve
- Obedience
- Open-mindedness
- Openness
- Optimism
- Order
- Organization
- Originality
- Outlandishness
- Outrageousness
- Passion
- Peace
- Perceptiveness
- Perfection
- Perkiness

- Perseverance
- Persistence
- Persuasiveness
- Philanthropy
- Piety
- Playfulness
- Pleasantness
- Pleasure
- Poise
- Polish
- Popularity
- Potency
- Power
- Practicality
- Pragmatism
- Precision
- Preparedness
- Presence
- Privacy
- Proactivity
- Professionalism
- Prosperity
- Prudence
- Punctuality
- Purity
- Realism
- Reason
- Reasonableness
- Recognition
- Recreation
- Refinement
- Reflection
- Relaxation
- Reliability
- Religiousness
- Resilience
- Resolution
- Resolve
- Resourcefulness
- Respect
- Rest
- Restraint
- Reverence
- Richness
- Rigor
- Sacredness
- Sacrifice
- Sagacity
- Saintliness
- Sanguinity
- Satisfaction
- Security
- Self-control
- Selflessness
- Self-reliance
- Sensitivity
- Sensuality
- Serenity
- Service
- Sexuality
- Sharing
- Shrewdness

STEP 1: DISCOVER YOU

- Significance
- Silence
- Silliness
- Simplicity
- Sincerity
- Skillfulness
- Solidarity
- Solitude
- Soundness
- Speed
- Spirit
- Spirituality
- Spontaneity
- Spunk
- Stability
- Stealth
- Stillness
- Strength
- Structure
- Success
- Support
- Supremacy
- Surprise
- Sympathy
- Synergy
- Teamwork
- Temperance
- Thankfulness
- Thoroughness
- Thoughtfulness
- Thrift
- Tidiness
- Timeliness
- Traditionalism
- Tranquility
- Transcendence
- Trust
- Trustworthiness
- Truth
- Understanding
- Unflappability
- Uniqueness
- Unity
- Usefulness
- Utility
- Valor
- Variety
- Victory
- Vigor
- Vitality
- Warmth
- Watchfulness
- Wealth
- Willingness
- Winning
- Wisdom
- Wonder
- Youthfulness
- Zeal

It's important to note, some values will stay with us for our entire lives, while others will likely change over time. They're a reflection of the person you are right now, and as you move through various stages of life, your values will likely change.

What are you passionate about?

The most crucial part of launching a new venture is determining what kind of business is right for you. This will make or break your business. Anyone can open an ice cream shop, but if you hate working in the summer, don't enjoy talking to people and prefer cake to ice cream, why would you do it?

According to many studies, 9 out of 10 new businesses are doomed to fail. Why? Let's say your friend starts a small business selling handmade bookmarks, and the business booms. Seeing that makes you want to create a bookmark business of your own, so you spend hundreds of dollars buying supplies and learning how to make the bookmarks, only for the business to collapse, leaving you disheartened and disappointed.

To save you from that emotional rollercoaster and financial distress, here's some advice: *don't assume one person's success will guarantee yours*. Find out what you are enthusiastic about - what inspires you. Success requires **passion**, and if your heart's not in it, your customers will know.

Instead, realise that you don't have an artistic bone in you. Maybe you delight in the art of baking more than painting and drawing. Perhaps you find joy in the measuring of ingredients and meticulously decorating your cake and other baked goods. Your success will depend on doing what exhilarates you as you strive to be more competent at it.

Here's the tricky part. **How** do you know what you're passionate about?

Journal Activity 2

1. What do you love to do that gives you the greatest joy? Think about activities you do that leave you feeling energised. Are there certain things you do where time just disappears because you love doing it so much? Think in terms of work, home, family, relationships, friends, hobbies - anything in your life that makes you happy.

2. What jobs/tasks are you good at? Think of things that come naturally to you and that people often praise you for. Maybe you don't 'love' doing them, but take the time to recognise the things you do well. This can be anything, even something as simple as starting conversations with strangers or arranging pillows on chaise lounges!

> 3 What do you hate to do? What do you procrastinate about getting done? Often procrastinating means we're just not interested in doing it. After all, you don't procrastinate binge-watching your favourite TV show, do you?
>
> 4 What are you passionate about? Is it family, animals, the environment, healthy food, chemical-free cleaning? Think of things that come up in conversations with friends and family that you just have to share your views on.
>
> 5 What would you do if you knew you could not fail?
>
> ***

What is your purpose?

Besides creating a steady side income, there are likely other reasons you have decided to invest your time, money, and efforts into starting a new venture.

Unlike many full-time, permanent jobs that restrict you to the routine dictated by your employer, a side hustle provides you with a creative space that allows you to explore your purpose. Perhaps you want to promote good health, give more to the environment or create fundraisers for meaningful causes. There must be a force driving you to pursue your passions, pushing you to a goal. Our aim here is to discover this purpose and monetise it.

STEP 1: DISCOVER YOU

Go back to your notebook and answer the following questions.

Journal Activity 3

1 What would you do with your time if money wasn't an issue?

2 What would you do to serve others (give back to the community) if money wasn't an issue?

3 What kind of people would you like to help? How have your life challenges and experiences equipped you to serve others?

4 What is your 'why'? Write down all your aims, objectives, and purposes of why you want to begin a new enterprise. Envision a scenario where your business is prospering in the future. What, other than financial security, do you derive from that?

Ask yourself the real reason you have decided to embark on a new career path. Finding the true motive behind this new beginning will help you determine your goals and will centre your attention on the objective in mind.

***

What would make you happy?

Now that you have done a bit of self-discovery, it's time to analyse your answers.

These answers - the ones that make up your core values - will help you determine what truly makes you happy and brings contentment as well as exuberance into your life.

> *Journal Activity 4*
>
> Take out your notebook again. Write out the top five 'things that you love to do,' that you listed in Activity 2, Question 1. Next to each of these things, write down which of your values that this activity fulfils. These values can be found from your answers in Activity 1, Question 3. Next, write down some money-making ideas from each of these five activities. You may find, combining some of your favourite activities will give you something unique that you can offer the world.
>
> ***

While it's true that the journey to a side hustle is full of doubts, I'm certain that you might have a few creative thoughts knocking around in your brain. It's also quite all right - and completely normal - if the ideas elude you in the beginning. Being scared is expected, but don't let yourself fixate on those negative thoughts. Don't allow yourself to be held back by anxiety.

While there's still a great deal to consider, I would advise you to keep coming back to these questions to keep you on the right path. Be persistent. Following your core values, passion and purpose will lead you to discover precisely what side hustle is perfect for YOU.

Chapter Summary

- Understanding your values, what makes you 'tick' will ultimately help you make better decisions about the direction of your side hustle.

- Discover what you are genuinely passionate about. Follow your heart.

- Design your side hustle in a way that gives you purpose in life. It's not all about the money! How can you create a career AND fulfil your ultimate goals at the same time?

In the next chapter, we're looking at key factors for you to consider before deciding the direction of your side hustle. In the planning phase, we are in charge of the path we take, so let's mould it to suit our lifestyle choices.

STEP TWO
Consider what you want

"The key to accepting responsibility for your life is to accept the fact that your choices, every one of them, are leading you inexorably to either success or failure, however you define those terms." **– Neal Boortz**

Your business ultimately becomes the result of many, many small decisions. As you create your side-hustle, you inevitably come across obstacles. You will make decisions to overcome these obstacles. This, in effect, will create the structure of your business.

Before you kick things off, it's good to create a picture of what you want. Let's begin to consider a few important factors to properly envisage the underlying structure of your enterprise.

Who do you want to spend your time with?

As enticing as the idea might seem, it could become exhausting if you choose to work alone. Before you start to hire or contract co-workers out of desperation, perhaps you should consider *who* you want to work *with*. This is your business, and you have the ability to plan an environment that works best for you.

Your team will cultivate an environment that can directly affect your spirit and energy, which is why it's crucial to ensure that you are surrounded by hard-working people who are just as passionate as you are about the project and are willing to give their best. You will, undoubtedly, work better if you have surrounded yourself with people with positive energy.

For instance, Multi-Level Marketing (MLM) is all about working and coordinating with a team. At the end of the day, you are the one who will determine the direction of your business. It's up to you to choose a team that works for you, so create an atmosphere that suits your vision.

On the flip side of this are your customers. Who are your ideal clients? What types of people do you want to help? There are many ways to attract the right people to your business. Your prices, your branding, your services will attract certain personality types. You have the ability to create the business and vibe that attracts those you want to work with.

STEP 2: CONSIDER WHAT YOU WANT

Journal Activity 5

Grab your notebook and make a list of your ideal customers and your ideal contractors/employees/team. This could either be particular people you have in mind or characteristics and attributes of the people you're looking for. Deciding who you want to work with now could very well manifest the perfect people into your life.

***

What schedule do you want to work?

One of the perks that come with a side hustle is that you get to decide your working hours. Unlike your day job, a side hustle may not require you to work specific hours. You are the boss of your time and the one who determines how to spend it. So, ask yourself, *how many hours am I willing to put into it? What types of hours do I want to work?*

Perhaps you would like to work during school hours to ensure that your work fits around the time your children are at school, so you can devote more time to your kids when they get home. Maybe you're looking into a business that requires longer hours where the weekend is not off-limits. Would you be able to manage, or will it put a mental and physical strain on you? Is there a short-term and long-term plan for the management of your time? Moreover, what if the side hustle requires you to travel a lot? Is that something you'd like to do?

All of these are things you need to consider before jumping into a new business. Maybe you're already working around the clock, so it's important to examine how you will spend your days. You don't need to work so much that you mentally exert yourself to the breaking point.

The early days of a business bring a rush of adrenaline. You are happily working long hours and missing out on fun with friends on weekends because, in your view, you need to work all the time to succeed. However, keep in mind that your small-time side hustle could turn into a big-time business. After all, you're reading this book and considering all the right questions to create an opportunity that you will love building and nurturing for the rest of your life. But ask yourself if you will love it in 12 months' time when you can't make it to your child's soccer game, *again!* Short-term hustle is fine but consider the long game now before you're in deep.

Journal Activity 6

Take out your notebook and take note of what you do during an average day. Then, create your ideal day. How would you spend your days if you were in complete control? Is there a way that you can make your 'ideal day' the new norm?

***

STEP 2: CONSIDER WHAT YOU WANT

What skills can you capitalise on?

Possibly the best thing about side hustling is that it doesn't require you to *learn* a new skill. Just make a list of all the skills you're already brilliant at. Combine these skills with your core values, and you're onto something that will suit you!

Perhaps your desserts and sweets have always bagged compliments at family dinners, but you don't like the idea of spending your time in a shop all day. Make it a home-based baking business that requires pre-orders. If you find cooking the same things monotonous, create new menus every fortnight and alternate the available items. You are in charge of this business; make it suit your skills and your values.

Start out working with something you're good at, and see where it takes you.

Kristin Berry, the founder of Miss Design Berry, was working in pharmaceutical advertising when she opened up an Etsy shop in 2011 to make use of her graphic design skills to sell logo designs, illustrations, and more. She quickly realised that wedding products were selling like hotcakes, so she added her unique touch. Fast forward to today, she is close to having a million dollars in revenue, with up to 20 employees working remotely!

"There is no perfect time, perfect product, or perfect idea. The biggest thing I have learned during my adventures in owning a business is that most people don't start out with their whole business planned out." - **Kristin Berry**, *the founder of Miss Design Berry*

There are so many options to choose from. The entrepreneur market is exceptionally vast, diverse and accommodates individuals with various skill sets. Perhaps you don't have a skill, per se, but you're wonderful at bringing groups of people together. How can you use this 'skill' to create a hustle that suits you? Rather than jumping headfirst into an opportunity that sounds like fun, spend a reasonable amount of time on research and figure out what works best for you.

Journal Activity 7

Go back to your answers from Chapter 1. Have you begun to get a clearer picture of what you'd like to do? Are there ideas forming that combine your skills, core values and passion? Can you think of a way to change your initial ideas to suit the time schedule of your 'ideal day,' working with the 'ideal co-workers and clients'? Journal your thoughts. Hopefully, you have some great ideas brewing by now.

***

How do you want to give back?

You have probably heard the saying, "The secret to happiness is helping others." Your purpose, the driving force behind taking such a big step, is what has driven you this far. There is a reason why you're doing this. Maybe

STEP 2: CONSIDER WHAT YOU WANT

you want to give something to the world. As a famous Chinese proverb says,

"If you want happiness for an hour, take a nap. If you want happiness for a day, go fishing. If you want happiness for a year, inherit a fortune. If you want happiness for a lifetime, help somebody."

Perhaps you would like to become involved in philanthropy and charity, so to feed the hungry, you create a food-related business that offers local homeless shelters a percentage of your products. Or you would like to donate a portion of your sales to cancer patients or victims of domestic violence. Maybe you'd like to educate orphaned children. Perhaps you're a performer who would like to build a better world for children, so you employ your talents and expertise to create inspiring shows for schools. Maybe you want to build an animal shelter.

Entrepreneurship is your chance to choose a role that not only allows you to live a life without financial problems, but also give back to the world in a way that rewards you with more than money.

Journal Activity 8

Journal some thoughts. By now, you've possibly noticed a theme in many of your answers. These often come back to a singular purpose. Do you now have a clearer understanding of your purpose? Forget for a moment all the details of how you will achieve this. What is the overall life purpose you've identified? This is likely to be very simple. Write a brief sentence about what you want to do, what legacy you want to leave. If this is too hard, decide what you want to do this year. Ideas of what you're looking for here is: I want to teach people how to get out of poverty, or I want to inspire people to live a healthier life.

***

What can you learn from the past?

While it's great to keep in mind your strengths, you also need to be self-aware of your flaws and vulnerabilities before launching a start-up.

You might be working in a cubicle at the moment, having direct contact with only your supervisor and colleagues. This is a part of your job that you like as you feel productive on your own and don't like interruptions. However, when you start your side hustle, things are likely to change. You will probably have direct contact with your customers and, especially when you start small, you may be the recipient of all the complaints, issues, and problems.

It's important to consider the things that make you procrastinate, make you agitated, negatively affect your mood, or you *straight-up* hate doing. Here is your chance to cultivate a setting in which these things are minimised. Maybe you prefer the barrier from human interaction that the walls of your cubicle provides. Perhaps you appreciate that your energy is not being drained from socialising with many people during the day.

If you are the type of person who prefers to avoid customer interaction, you can opt for a side hustle with a secretary who will handle all this for you. They can arrange your bookings, negotiate with clients, and handle complaints and anything else related to human interaction while you simply show up and clean empty offices for businesses during the night.

Alternatively, maybe there's something that annoys you that you believe annoys a lot of people. Could you invent a solution to this problem? Most inventions *solve a problem*. Does your personal gripe offer a business opportunity?

> ## Journal Activity 9
>
> Make a list of things that regularly irritate you, work that you constantly procrastinate about and situations that can quickly deflate your mood. You may like to brainstorm a little about how your personal 'gripe' can be monetised.
>
> ***

It's quite normal to feel overwhelmed at this point, but I advise you to be cautious and check off everything on the list before you turn your life around. There's a common saying in business, "proper planning prevents piss poor performance." I'd comment here that it should actually be "proper preparation prevents piss poor performance." Planning involves the process of deciding on all the details before you do it. This book is all about preparation, which is the act of getting ready and organising your thoughts before making exact plans.

No business opportunity will be perfect, and no one can guarantee that you will be headline news someday like other famous CEOs. Nevertheless, finding the right balance that ticks all the boxes will get you on the fast track to success. When you truly enjoy working on your side hustle, your enthusiasm will naturally shine through and will be evident to your customers, who will happily root for you.

Understanding all these factors will not only help your business to develop and thrive but will also establish your self-awareness, which will, in turn, grow your business.

Chapter Summary

- Before we get started, let's plan a side hustle that will ultimately suit our lifestyle. In life, we often fit life in around our day job, so let's find a business that creates your preferred lifestyle.

- Choose a style of business that allows you to work with the people you want to work with.

- Choose a style of business that will afford you the flexibility to spend your time however you wish. Whilst this may not be the case at first, ensure that the long-term plan suits your needs.

- What skills do you have that you're already good at? How can you use these skills to your advantage?

- How can you use your side hustle to give back?

- Choose a work situation that gives you peace. You don't want to work in an environment that regularly triggers negative emotions.

In the next chapter, we'll discuss the types of businesses in which to create your side hustle.

STEP THREE

Understand your options

"So often people are working hard at the wrong thing. Working on the right thing is probably more important than working hard."
- Caterina Fake, Flickr Co-Founder

Having considered many key factors involved in establishing your business, you've come to another roadblock. *What type of business model will I follow?* This chapter is a brief introduction to some of the types suitable as a side hustle.

Trading hours for dollars

Money is an abstract concept. To put it simply, although money might only be *printed paper*, it holds substantial sway over our daily life. In the words of Joe Dominguez and Vicki Robin in their book, *Your Money or Your Life*, money is something we trade our life energy for. This life energy is parallel to our time on Earth and involves numerous hours each day managing a workload for the money needed to pay for both necessities and things that bring us pleasure. We're spending all these hours every day to gain peace of mind, while ironically, we're missing major events, family dinners, and milestones.

As an employee, you are inevitably trading hours for dollars. You start your day at 9am, you leave at 5pm, and you are paid an hourly rate for that time. Your earning potential is limited to the number of hours you can work each week. As an entrepreneur, you have more choices. You are the sole owner of the money you receive in exchange for the hours and labour. You can choose how many hours you work. You can choose the dollar value you place on an hour of your time.

There are significant drawbacks to this style of business, and yet it is the most common. The obvious drawback is that you **don't** have enough time. Sure, for someone whose parents left them a trust fund or relative left them a large inheritance, leaving their day-to-day job to pursue a business of their own might be a piece of cake. But for the rest of us who have bills to pay and who can't leave our current job, a side hustle might take months or even years to be fully realised and successful. Quite an extended period. So, what are your choices?

Well, for example, instead of consulting one-to-one, you can consider group coaching. Perhaps you can create a high ticket offer that allows you to generate income quickly and allow you more freedom from the day job.

Many entrepreneurs use their skills to develop online programs that can create consistent income.

In the beginning, you will very likely be trading a lot of hours for a small amount of dollars, but if you'd like to escape from this restrictive business model, you can begin the process of building residual programs to really leverage your skills and maximise your income-earning ability.

Passive income

Is the prospect of adding more hours to your already heavy workload a little terrifying? Are you the kind of person who absolutely dreads the idea of spending more time on the clock yet wants to earn extra money?

Having extra cash to bolster your emergency savings, found a start-up, or invest for retirement is an attractive concept, but you're already working 'round the clock, *so how on Earth can you earn extra money?* Passive income is key if you fancy the financial freedom of making your own choices!

Passive income is money earned from an investment with little or no ongoing effort involved. The creation of passive income most likely consists of an upfront investment of time and money. Unlike trading time for money, which is an *active income*, passive income, has the potential for unlimited earning.

If you're wondering how to make passive income, there are a number of ways.

- **Online businesses:** Opening an Etsy or eBay store or a shop on Shopify is an excellent way of generating passive income. Creating information products or online courses is also widely popular. Getting the business up and running is more demanding during the initial period. This stage requires more time, effort, and labour, as well as a substantial investment in the beginning.

- **Short or long-term rental income:** You could rent out your house as a permanent rental or rent it to popular websites like Airbnb and Vrbo for shorter time increments. If, for instance, you want to go on holiday, you can rent out your home while you're gone. Obviously, there are some drawbacks and risks, including security costs and, well, you're letting strangers stay in your home, but it could result in passive income. Investing in rental properties is also an effective way to earn a passive income.

- **Affiliate marketing:** Promoting third-party products can create income for you while you're sleeping. Let's take the example of Christine. Christine is an affiliate blogger, meaning that she inserts her affiliate links (Amazon, eBay, etc.) into her blogposts. She also shares the links on her social media platforms, and all of this earns her a stable side income. When visitors on her blog and social media click on those links, she generates passive income. This can take a bit of time to set up; however, writing blogs about topics you enjoy could become quite lucrative.

There are many other options, including peer-to-peer lending, dividend stocks, flipping retail products, creating an app or writing a book.

The drawback of passive income is that it often works at a snail's pace. You need to build a following to be able to generate revenue through affiliate links, online stores, or frequent marketing to ensure your house attracts customers. The advantage, however, is long-term passive income, whereby you put in the work to create the product and then reap the rewards for years to come.

Network Marketing

Network Marketing is a business model popular among people who are looking for a flexible, part-time business. Network Marketing depends upon a network of distributors to expand a business. This business model relies on person-to-person sales by independent agents and representatives, who often choose to work from home. It is a simple practice where a business rewards its distributors for every person they bring into the business. There are many types of Network Marketing, including single-tier Network Marketing, two-tier Network Marketing, and Multi-Level Marketing (MLM). The advantages of MLM or network-based marketing are that it is flexible, doesn't cost a lot, and has an organisational hierarchy. While Network and Multi-Level Marketing programs have been accused of scamming consumers and of being pyramid schemes, there are differences between pyramid schemes and Network Marketing. While it's true that there is an organisational hierarchy that allows the agents to enjoy more benefits than their downline members, Network Marketing is still very much a legitimate business framework that offers genuine products and services sold to target audiences and consumers.

Journal Activity 10

Make a note of the type of business you're considering. How can you create passive income with your ideas so far? Which business model are you leaning towards?

***

STEP 3: UNDERSTAND YOUR OPTIONS

Chapter Summary

- Choose a style of business that you are comfortable working with.

- Trading hours for dollars is the most common way to make an income; however, will this achieve your long-term goals?

- Building opportunities for passive income may take time, but this may give you the long-term results you desire.

- Leverage affiliate marketing to make extra income in your field of expertise.

- Network Marketing is almost a ready-made business that could help kick-start your aspirations.

In the next chapter, we'll discuss what's holding you back. Why do you keep putting off building the life you dream of?

STEP FOUR
Overcome your obstacles

*"Obstacles are those frightful things you see when you take your eyes off your goal." - **Henry Ford***

Starting a business endeavour is an exciting decision. You're essentially freeing yourself from the expectations of the world and deciding your future. It's not all fun and games, though. The journey is riddled with roadblocks. Uncertainty and anxiety are quite normal emotions to experience when it comes to launching a new business.

Will it work out? What if it gets tainted with a bad review? What if I don't stand out, and my business is lost in a sea of others? These and a million other questions are swirling inside your head, filling you with dread and apprehension.

The concept of a side hustle creates many mindset hurdles. You derive comfort from the traditional work environment. A side business requires you to leap out of your comfort zone. We have been bred to live and survive in a traditional environment, which is why the idea of working on our own terms fills us with internal conflicts and doubt.

In this chapter, we will explore many fundamental factors that may be holding you back. Whilst we can't deal with solving all of these problems here, becoming aware of them is the first step.

Fear

Fear is a survival instinct, but it often holds people back from progress in many areas of their lives. Overthinking can consume the rational part of the brain, forcing you to unnecessarily dissect and over-scrutinise elements of your plan, resulting in fear of rejection, fear of the business failing, fear of letting people down and wasting time, effort and money. Realistically speaking, we cannot eliminate this emotion; what we can do is embrace it and face it head-on. There is no way to experiment and take risks in life without the feeling of self-doubt creeping in, so give yourself a break. Even if the worst-case scenario happens, it likely won't be as bad as you've imagined, and you will find a solution to it.

This fear is preventing you from following through with your goals. Veronica Roth, the writer of the *Divergent* series, said, "Becoming fearless isn't the point. That's

STEP 4: OVERCOME YOUR OBSTACLES

impossible. It's learning how to control your fear, and how to be free from it." Despite the thoughts of self-doubt and negative outcomes building a nest in your brain, take the plunge anyway. This is what we call courage. Think about it for a moment. Which is better? Taking a risk or doing absolutely nothing? What if the outcome is not as bad as what you'd feared? What if your fears don't materialise?

The only secret to moving forward is to be more powerful than your fears, to change your mindset regarding the fear of failure or disappointment. Acknowledge the fact that whilst there might be many victories, both small and large; there will also be failures. However, when you fail, instead of having regrets, choose to learn from the failures, as this will prevent you from making the same mistakes again. Stand up to your fears. This display of courage will boost your self-confidence, and, in time, you will begin taking risks without overthinking them. The more you do something that has risk, the less risky it becomes and the closer you get to conquering your fear!

Journal Activity 11

Is there a dream or passion in your life that you've always wanted to follow, but something has held you back? What is the fear that's stopping you from chasing your dream? How do you feel about making changes in your life? What scares you the most about stepping out of your comfort zone?

***

Money and time

Are you using time or money as an excuse?

Your day job might be paying for all your essentials and necessities but in this economy, beginning a side hustle is a game-changer that can help you achieve your goals, giving you the extra cash that brings along the financial freedom you have always wanted. But here's the catch: *How to make time for a side hustle when you are already drowning in work from your day job? How much money should you invest? What if the side hustle is not a hit, and you suffer the loss?* These questions probably haunt your mind.

When it comes to money, it's wise to limit the amount you're willing to invest in the side business. Don't be too idealistic when it comes to investment. You need to be logical and ensure that you don't throw all of your money into the side hustle.

Create a budget. Make a rational and reasonable plan. Take into account all the factors that constitute the business, including the tools, investments, advertisement and marketing, etc. Next, categorise each of the sections and allot money from the total budget to each. Once you have a budget, be sure to set the funds aside and use this money only for your side hustle.

Time is also a valuable commodity, more valuable than any currency. All the more reason not to waste it on your corporate job! It might be a little unnerving for you to make time for something so new and risky, but don't let the fear hinder you. Be prepared to give up some luxuries when you're first creating your side hustle, because this business will eventually allow you to manage your own time. Whilst we all love to say, 'I don't have time,' you are ultimately in charge of your time and how you spend it.

Journal Activity 12

Are you using time or money as an excuse? Is there another fear behind these excuses?

***

Procrastination

When it comes to getting things done, do you constantly procrastinate? There's a good solution to procrastination, and it's pretty simple. Think about the things you procrastinate about. Are they the 'fun' things you like to do, or are they the difficult or mundane tasks you'd rather avoid? Obviously, it's the latter. Nobody ever procrastinates or delays doing the things they want to do. Here's where Chapters 1 and 2 can really come into play. Choose a working environment that you love. Choose to do tasks that you really enjoy. In any business, there will be tasks we don't like, but don't let those hold you back from the ones that bring you pleasure. As soon as you can afford it, delegate the tasks that are holding you back, overwhelming you and slowing progress.

Journal Activity 13

Is there something in your life that you constantly put off doing? Why do you think you do this? How do you think you can avoid this problem?

***

Imposter Syndrome

If you're starting your journey to a side hustle, you might begin to feel Imposter Syndrome creeping up on you. It's not easy striking out on your own based solely on your talents, so you've likely crossed paths with this emotion.

Imposter Syndrome is a recurring fear of being a fraud or thought of as a fraud, and causes us to doubt our skills and abilities. This syndrome makes you think less of yourself, so you dwell on self-doubt and wonder if it is futile to try to swim in a bigger pond. If you allow the feeling to remain, it will undoubtedly take over and derail your mental and emotional energy, and you will be stranded. It could paralyse any of the progress your business makes because it causes you to believe that you are undeserving of your success, so it could prevent forward progress.

Take heart, though; you are not alone in this. In fact, it's much more common than you might think. Whether you are a budding entrepreneur or an established CEO, these feelings take root deep inside, then try to crawl their way to the top and override your confidence.

STEP 4: OVERCOME YOUR OBSTACLES

Maya Angelou once commented about herself:

"I have written 11 books, but each time I think, 'Uh oh, they're going to find out now. I've run a game on everybody, and they're going to find me out."

So, the question arises, *How can you stop feeling like an imposter and accept your progress and victories?* Here are some recommendations:

- Stop comparing yourself with others. Everyone has their own journey to becoming who they are. Others' struggles have been entirely different from yours, so comparing yourself with someone who has been in the business for ten years and is more successful than you is absolutely nonsensical. You need to direct your focus on your own business, the doors you still need to open, and the steps you need to climb on the ladder rather than exhausting your mental energy on drawing comparisons.

- You don't have to be an expert. There are steps in a journey. Don't expect to become a shining star at the first step. Work on the quality, be patient, and appreciate your progress, no matter how small it may be.

- When Imposter Syndrome creeps in, remind yourself that you are steps ahead of many people. Whilst you may not know it all, you do know more than some. It's to those people that you can truly be of assistance.

Journal Activity 14

What steps do you think you can take to overcome Imposter Syndrome?

***

The people around you

More often than not, we rely on the people around us to be our support system, to encourage us and stick with us through thick and thin, especially when it comes to taking significant risks like starting a side business. It's human nature to crave validation from those who you care about. Be aware that you may not be supported.

If you're worried that you might be embarking on this journey alone, take some time out to communicate. Communication is key, so lay down your plans to your significant other, kids, or anyone else in your life who you feel should know. Have a healthy discussion, ask them their opinions. Approach your friends and consult them. Let them know that their support means a lot to you. If you still can't find the support you feel you need, seek out local groups and business people who inspire you. Find yourself some cheerleaders wherever you can. This is how you free yourself from the thoughts of loneliness and feeling misunderstood. Having a cheerleader on your side can help you overcome the fear of letting others down.

STEP 4: OVERCOME YOUR OBSTACLES

Journal Activity 15

Make a list of the people in your life who can be your cheerleaders. If you can't think of anyone, what steps can you take to find some?

***

Belief in yourself

*"No such thing as the right time, situation, or place. You have all it takes. Just dig within. Exhume all the greatness inside of you and transform the world with an inexhaustible drive and without fear of limitations." - **Chinonye J. Chidolue***

Starting a business is not like trying out a new recipe or painting your room. It's not for the faint-hearted. You need to be confident enough to go all out in the entrepreneur world. You have motivated yourself enough to let the idea of starting your business build a home inside your heart. Imagining a thriving business and satisfied clients is keeping you going, but remember, believing in yourself and your abilities is ultimately the only thing that will push you further along this path.

Stay committed and persistent. Be willing to experiment and fail and learn from those failures. Surround yourself with cheerleaders because it does not matter how many people are against you; it's the ones who choose to stick by you that make the difference in your life and career.

> ## Journal Activity 16
>
> Recall a time that you felt confident and successful. Write down the steps you took to reach this point.
>
> ***

If you genuinely want to become a side hustler, commit to believing in yourself. Drop the constant self-doubt and reach for your dreams. Back yourself! You've got this!

As I mentioned at the start of this chapter, identifying what's holding you back is just the beginning. And of course, I know that telling yourself to believe in yourself doesn't make it instantly so. Instead of letting these fears stop you in your tracks or cause you to waste time overthinking, attack them head-on. Read books, listen to podcasts or invest in self-help programs that can assist you in becoming the version of you who is running a successful business! Educating yourself in the skills that you're lacking may become the most beneficial investment that you'll ever make of your time and money.

Confront your fears and stop letting them be your excuses!

STEP 4: OVERCOME YOUR OBSTACLES

Journal Activity 17

Grab your trusty notepad.

1. Write yourself a list of obstacles you've had in your life and how you've overcome them. Large or small, we've all overcome an obstacle that allows us to be in the position we're in today.

2. Make a list of what's holding you back. Is it just time and money (excuse), or is there a real fear you're ignoring? Identify the fear.

3. What changes can you make to overcome your fears?

4. What strategies, activities or books could help?

5. Make a plan to start implementing these ideas.

***

Chapter Summary

- Everyone has fear when stepping out of their comfort zone. How you handle this fear will pave the way for your future goals.

- Are you letting the practicalities of time and money hold you back? If you really want to make this work, create your own opportunities.

- If procrastination is holding you back, what can you do to resolve it? Nobody procrastinates when they want to binge-watch their favourite series.

- Imposter Syndrome: acknowledge that it's a real thing and work out what you need to do to overcome it. Do you need to learn more about your field, or is it simply about changing your mindset?

- Don't listen to those who don't support you. Instead, find yourself some inspirational friends and cheerleaders.

- Believe in yourself. Seriously, you're amazing!

In the next chapter, let's make some decisions. Decide on what it is that you really want to do in your side hustle.

STEP FIVE
Make some decisions

"Your life changes the moment you make a new, congruent, and committed decision." – **Tony Robbins**

The time has come to make some decisions. Before jumping into a side hustle with both feet, you've got some serious decisions to make. Don't be anxious. After all, you've done all this work so far, and you're now prepared to make some informed decisions.

In previous chapters, you've established a LOT, or at least started analysing your feelings towards the type of side hustle you'd like to create. You now have an understanding of how your core values, passion and purpose can unite to create something well suited to you. We've started the thoughts on the hours you'd like to work, the people you'd like to work with, the skills you have to use and the ways you'd like to give back to the world. We've also discussed the things you don't like doing; recognising these can be imperative to your success.

During Chapter 3, we briefly discussed the types of business you may wish to invest your time in. Then, we uncovered the underlying reasons that many people hold themselves back. Both of these chapters may require some further research or self-development, but this brief overview may have opened your eyes to what's possible and why you haven't yet taken the leap.

How much time can you commit?

It shouldn't come as a surprise that starting a new career on the side will require a lot of effort and, yes, time. This time doesn't magically appear out of thin air to solve all your problems. A fairy godmother will not appear and wave her wand, proclaim her magical words, and add more hours to your day. You'll have to actively take time out of your hectic schedule to fit in the work required for the side gig.

You may already be working around the clock on your day job, and the idea of making time for a side hustle, your significant other, and the kids can mentally strain you. How can you possibly make time for all of that and yourself with only 24 hours in a day?

The solution, whilst not easy, is simple: you have to make the time, one way or another. You cannot avoid it if you want to be successful in this fast-paced, technology-driven world.

STEP 5: MAKE SOME DECISIONS

"The key is not to prioritise what's on your schedule, but to schedule your priorities." - **Steven Covey**

Create a plan and use time management techniques, such as the single-task technique that has been proven to amplify productivity. Instead of multitasking, focusing on doing one thing at a time helps you get more done in less time since you are paying more attention to your work, and therefore are working smarter rather than just harder.

There are many ways we can 'find time' in our schedules: wake up before the family and power through some work, read or work on your daily commute, use lunch breaks and waiting time to promote on social media or respond to clients. The side hustle is a hustle. If you're not willing to hustle, your progress will be slow.

"The secret of getting ahead is getting started. The secret of getting started is breaking your complex overwhelming tasks into smaller manageable tasks, and then starting on the first one." - **Mark Twain**

Journal Activity 18

Create a schedule for your side-hustle. When will you be able to set aside time to be focused? What are you willing to give up while you're building your dream?

***

What's the long-term goal?

The initial start-up phase of any business requires more work than the day-to-day activities. Continuously working during all your spare moments isn't what creating a side-hustle is about. It's a good idea to make a decision about what your ongoing, long-term time commitment goals are. Perhaps you want to create a side hustle that ultimately requires only 4 hours a day. It's entirely possible to create this, especially when you're at the beginning and deciding the direction you want your business to take. It's easy to get carried away by the grind culture, but you (or any aspiring or established entrepreneur) should not equate hours worked with success.

Equating hours with the level of success is a false equivalence. It's irrational and, quite frankly, illogical to demand 5+ hours of daily work from yourself while juggling a day job, and you'll likely experience burnout. As much as YouTube motivational gurus and entrepreneurs like to encourage their audience to work 20+ hours a day, research suggests that working long hours can be detrimental to your productivity and overall well-being.

What types of hours do you want to work?

Whilst you may have grand plans of becoming a life coach, what type of hours will this require you to work? Will you be on the phone every evening with your clients instead of spending time with your family? Perhaps you're thinking of opening a brick and mortar shop but prefer to work only during school hours. These are the types of practicalities you need to consider before embarking on your new venture. If your work involves hours you don't want to work in the long-term, think outside the box and create opportunities that work with your lifestyle goals. Perhaps you can turn your coaching into an online program and create a team that speaks to your clients on your behalf, or maybe your shop can be a combination of online and pop-up stores.

While stepping into the vast world of entrepreneurship might seem like a daunting endeavour, think of all the benefits you can reap once your business prospers! Use this time of planning to create the type of business you will enjoy for a long time.

Journal Activity 19

What is the dream? How many hours will you work? Will you still have a day job? Create a schedule of your ideal day or week. Perhaps your workdays will be spent with a laptop at the beach? Create a vision of how you will spend your time.

***

What does success look like to you?

We all have a different definition of success. For some, success might be reaching a specific amount of money in our bank account, owning our dream house, or going on holidays with our family without worrying about how much money is in our wallet. Even dreams that might seem small to other people, like finally hiring a house cleaner, might be one that you'd like to check off your list someday. Success is a personal decision, uniquely different for every individual.

When an entrepreneur embarks on a journey to begin their dream career, they always carry with them a vision, along with the objectives they aspire to achieve. Keeping the objectives in sight motivates you to work harder towards your goal, which is why it's imperative to ask yourself, *What does success mean to me?*

Is it extra cash on the side, financial freedom, more family time, fewer working hours, or freedom from corporate life?

The only person who can answer these questions is you.

Rather than tirelessly working on your side career, redefine what you want to be and envision what success means to you. *What do you hope to achieve by tirelessly working on another job?*

I can tell you that working endless hours on a side gig without a significant outcome should not be how you perceive success. Instead of focusing only on more cash, make a list of all that you hope to attain. This is a helpful exercise to determine your goals and can direct your focus on what you aspire to in life.

Journal Activity 20

At what point will you hit your first milestone of 'success'? Will it be booking a certain number of clients, earning a certain amount of money, creating a particular product? What is the 'big' success goal?

***

Chapter Summary

- Let's make some decisions about the direction our side hustle will go and how to make it suit the lifestyle we seek.

- Decide how much time you can really commit to your side hustle now, and make a plan on how you can most effectively utilise your time and skills.

- Ultimately, what's the long-term goal for your business and how much time do you want to be working on it?

- What type of hours do you want to work? Think outside the box to design the types of hours your business will require.

- Determine how you will define success. Will it be a specific dollar amount per week, a certain number of clients, or an hourly rate that you charge? Define your goal, so you'll know when you've made it.

In the next chapter, we'll go over a selection of tips that a large majority of entrepreneurs share. Listening to those who've done it before can make all the difference.

STEP SIX
Follow the leaders

"Find the smartest people you can and surround yourself with them." - ***Marissa Meyer***

It's easier to think of success as something that happened overnight, like an incredible windfall because you got lucky, as opposed to something that came about after years of hard work, all-nighters, and struggles that one might endure to become who and what they are.

Many aspiring entrepreneurs and founders have walked this road, even passed by the very hurdles that intimidate you. Many are taking the journey at the exact moment you're reading this book. Nearly 46.5 million people are embracing a side hustle in Canada and the United States. If you're wondering how you'll ever be able to compete and succeed in the harsh world of entrepreneurship and start-ups, there are hundreds of examples of projects that were started on the side that have grown into full-time, world-famous businesses. Facebook was a dorm room project. Instagram and Twitter weren't the centres of attention of their founders before they took the world by storm, and now these platforms have become a source of income for other entrepreneurs.

There is an abundance of roadmaps to guide you along the path of success. Thousands of books have been written by CEOs and millionaires about the steps they took along the way. Of course, every individual encounters their own hardships and circumstances, but consider reading some of their stories to help you come up with your own solutions

The following is a selection of lessons I've learned along the way – from people a lot smarter than I am!

Your mindset is the key

Our mindset has incredible power over our daily life. Whether positive or negative, your mindset is reflected in your mood and in the behaviours in which you engage when you want to achieve greatness. Start imagining possibilities instead of letting negativity invade your mind.

We could discuss for hours how to improve your mindset. Develop a growth mindset, learn from mistakes, visualise your dreams, set your goals, surround yourself with like-minded people. The list goes on and on.

Reading books and blogs, and listening to audiobooks or podcasts are both ideal ways to learn from the experts without breaking the bank. There's a wealth of knowledge out there for the taking. Use any spare moment you have to expand your knowledge and create the mindset of an entrepreneur.

Success is rarely the result of dumb luck. It depends on how willing you are to make changes within yourself to achieve it. With the right approach to life, I believe anyone can be prosperous.

Get out of your own way

It's time to stop overthinking and second-guessing yourself.

> *"Thinking too much leads to paralysis by analysis. It's important to think things through, but many use thinking as a means of avoiding action."* – **Robert Herjavek**

Here's my favourite tip to help you out: use Mel Robbins' *5 Second Rule*.

Mel Robbins, acclaimed author and renowned motivational speaker, came up with an effective way to accomplish a task. According to her,

> *"If you have an instinct to act on a goal, you must physically move within 5 seconds or your brain will kill it."*

When you have a desire to act on a goal, count 5-4-3-2-1 and then **DO IT**, otherwise your brain will stubbornly refuse to commit to the action. Henceforth, when you're free - maybe it's a small lunch break, a commute, etc. - and feel like working on your side gig, carry it out before your brain hacks off your willingness to move. This is a very helpful trick to push yourself to actually work on your goal, as the counting allows you to focus your mental energy on the task only, motivating you to act and thus leading you one step closer to your goal.

Take time out for yourself

It's easy to get carried away by the *grind culture* that motivational speakers like to chat about: working 20 hours a day until you achieve your dreams… but I absolutely despise that idea. Your corporate job may have already made you miserable; you rarely have time to eat anything but an apple during the day. You're already worked up and burnt out. You don't need to tangle yourself up in the web of the grind culture.

There's a better way to do things. You can work and make time for yourself as well. If you suffer burnout from mental and physical exertion, then you likely won't achieve much. You need to rejuvenate your mind and body. If you're wondering how to manage that, I'll tell you. *Discipline.* If you follow through with a routine and remember to save some time for yourself, then believe me, you will be able to succeed without locking yourself in a mental cage with worry and anxiety.

Formulate a schedule and allot some time to yourself. Whether it's 45 minutes for a long, hot bath, a shopping trip with a friend, reading 100 pages of your current novel, meditating, journaling or just a relaxing nap, find the time. Decide what takes your mind off of the day's travails and lose yourself in that activity.

STEP 6: FOLLOW THE LEADERS

Don't ignore your relationships

I have repeatedly emphasised the need to make the goals and keep them in your sights. Remember why you are starting this journey.

The corporate job may leave you no time for your family. Don't create a side hustle that does this as well. One of the perks of being a side hustler is the freedom of time it ultimately gives you. So, while you work, don't ignore those who care so much about you.

You don't have to be unique

There is always pressure, especially in the world of business, to be unique, to *think out of the box*.

Once you dig a little deeper into the stories of others, you'll realise that most people who exceeded the benchmark and formed one of their own are folks who didn't come up with a unique or original idea. Most of them spun a twist on an idea that already existed.

For instance, MySpace existed before Facebook was founded. But Mark Zuckerberg managed to create a social media that aligned better with the young audience. Subsequently, the popularity of MySpace declined, as it was clouded over by Facebook.

Similarly, and contrary to popular belief, Henry Ford, founder of Ford Motor Company, did not invent the car. He revolutionised the industry by making the automobile accessible to the masses, instead of a luxury meant only for the rich. There are countless other examples: Bill Gates, Elon Musk, Sara Blakely. The list is long. They all took a poorly executed idea, twisted it into a shape they liked, and ran with it. You can do that too!

Remember that uniqueness is not synonymous with being original. Take an idea that's already out there, mould it however you'd like and add your personal touch to it, then present it to your audience. No two brains work the same way or have the same potential. Find an existing idea and create your version of it. Find *your* **genius zone**!

Journal Activity 21

Create yourself a list of books you want to read. Who's story could help your journey. If you're stuck for ideas, download the free ebook available at the beginning of the book. What can you learn from others? Do you want information from people in the same field? Do you need to work on your fears and uncover what's really holding you back? Do you want to understand more about developing your entrepreneurial mindset? There's a wealth of information out there that's yours for the taking.

***

STEP 6: FOLLOW THE LEADERS

Chapter Summary

- You don't have to re-invent the wheel! Use the path others have taken to lead you to success.

- Mindset, mindset, mindset! It really is the key to your success.

- Remember, as you hustle, you still have to take care of yourself. Take time out and do things that nurture your heart and soul.

- In the craziness of the hustle, always remember your family needs your time too.

- You don't have to be unique – leverage others' ideas and make them your own.

Congratulations, you made it! I hope you've been absorbing ideas about how you can turn your passions, purpose and values into a profitable side hustle. Don't panic if you haven't yet solved your problems. It's a marathon, not a sprint.

Final words

"Build your own dreams, or someone else will hire you to build theirs." – **Farrah Gray**

Side hustle might sound like a precarious endeavour; however, everything in your life is a risk. Your next meal, your commute, going to work and leaving the house empty. After all, living every single day is about taking all kinds of big and small risks. So why not one that has the potential to turn your life around 180°, and for the better?

You see, our brain is a trickster. It seduces you with the idea of venturing into the world of side hustling, but at the same time, it lists all the reasons why you should not go for it. *It's risky. I don't have time. What will my friends & family think? What if I fail?* So many thoughts kicking around in your brain. But sit down for a minute and think about what your life will look like 20 years from now if nothing changes. Is it your dream to work a 9-5 job until the day you die? To let the corporate world prevent you from making your dreams come true? I doubt it.

Do not spend your life worrying about the next paycheck. We all fantasise about freeing ourselves from the constraints of the corporate world and being at peace with our choices in our twilight years, so take the first step. I agree it's the hardest one, but it's the one that will ultimately push you to begin the journey. Don't let fear or pessimism keep you from your dreams. You don't want to look back 20 years from now, your heart filled with regret, and ask yourself, *What if?* Get up and make your dreams come true!

Journal Activity 22

Write your 'What if?'. Take out your notebook and answer the questions:

1 What will my life be like in ten years if nothing changes.

2 Now, what will my life be like if I'm living the life of my dreams?

SPECIAL BONUS

FREE Workbook including Journaling Activities for choosing your Side Hustle PLUS over 120 Inspirational Books to add to your Reading List

Get FREE unlimited access to this AND all of my new books by joining our fan base!

SCAN WITH YOUR CAMERA OR GO TO
bit.ly/SideHustleWorkbook

REFERENCES

E., Darma. (2020, February 27). 5 reasons why you need to start a side hustle right now. Retrieved from https://elisedarma.com/blog/start-side-hustle

Griffith, E. (2015, March 02). Startups are failing because they make products no one wants. Retrieved from https://fortune.com/2014/09/25/why-startups-fail-according-to-their-founders/

Olito, F. (2020, March 31). 13 famous companies that started out as side hustles. Retrieved from https://www.businessinsider.com/companies-started-as-side-hustles-2019-

Lockert, M. (n.d.). 5 Entrepreneurs Who Took Their Side Hustle Full-Time. Retrieved from https://www.thebalancesmb.com/entrepreneurs-taking-side-hustles-full-time-4136679

Donnelly, G., By:, T. A., & Graeme Donnelly {"@context": "http://schema.org/". (2021, May 12). 7 important factors to consider before starting a business. Retrieved from https://startups.co.uk/strategy/7-important-factors-to-consider-before-starting-a-business/

Dropdesk. (2021, July 02). 101 Inspirational Quotes For Startups. Retrieved from https://drop-desk.com/blog/startup-quotes

Iny, D. (2016, August 23). Why You Can Never Stop Trading Time for Money (And What Can Do Instead). Retrieved from https://www.inc.com/danny-iny/why-you-can-never-stop-trading-time-for-money-and-what-can-do-instead.htm

Roth, J. (2012, May 18). Trading Time for Money. Retrieved from https://www.forbes.com/sites/moneybuilder/2012/05/16/trading-time-for-money/?sh=663ae6af5b8d

SoFi. (2021, July 22). How to Earn Residual Income. Retrieved from https://www.sofi.com/learn/content/ways-to-build-residual-income

What is network marketing? Definition and examples. (2019, September 29). Retrieved from https://marketbusinessnews.com/financial-glossary/network-marketing-definition/

Robinson, R. (n.d.). How to Start a Side Hustle While Keeping Your Day Job. Retrieved from https://www.thebalancesmb.com/how-to-start-a-side-business-while-keeping-your-day-job-4115403

4 Reasons You Need a Side Hustle: Discover. (2018, June 11). Retrieved from https://www.discover.com/online-banking/banking-topics/4-reasons-you-need-a-side-hustle/

Also available by **Kathy Shanks**...

Guided Journaling is available worldwide as print or ebook at Amazon, Booktopia, Barnes & Noble and all good bookstores.

Also available in Australia from **turtlepublishing.com.au**

Inside this book you'll discover how to use my method of journaling to:

- Work towards creating balance for heart, mind, body and soul without sacrificing career and relationships
- Create rituals that help you develop gratitude
- Use daily affirmations to practice positivity and manifest your future dreams
- Discover strategies to improve your relationships, build your life mission, start a side hustle, discover yourself, develop self-love, improve your health AND improve your mindset

It seems too good to be true, right! Organising your thoughts and dreams in 10-20 minutes a day can be that one simple change that actually makes your dreams become a reality.

Make your journal your safe haven, a place of nurturing for you to come and reflect, clear your mind, set goals, develop gratitude, make plans, dream, and take steps towards the future that has always seemed just out of reach.

> Please join our journaling community at
> **facebook.com/groups/kathyshanks**
> for exclusive insider access to updates and releases

Also available in the
Guided Journaling Series...

Journaling for a
Balanced Life with a
Health focus

Journaling for a
Balanced Life with a
Life Mission focus

Journaling for a
Balanced Life with a
focus on the **Heart**

Journaling for a
Balanced Life with a
Gratitude & **Manifest** focus

We have a selection of *journals* available worldwide as
print or ebook at Amazon, Booktopia,
Barnes & Noble and all good bookstores.
Also available in Australia from **turtlepublishing.com.au**